Places to Visit

Nick Bruce

There are many famous places to visit in the United States.

Have you been to the **Grand Canyon**? It is in Arizona.

UNITED STATES
★ **Grand Canyon**

The **Grand Canyon** is a deep valley with steep sides. In some places it is 18 miles wide. Other places are less than one mile wide.

Have you been to
Yellowstone
National Park?
It is in Wyoming,
Idaho, and Montana.

★Yellowstone
National Park
UNITED STATES

Yellowstone is the oldest National Park in the world. It is one of the largest safe areas for wildlife in the United States.

Have you been to
Niagara Falls?
It is in New York.

Niagara Falls

U N I T E D   S T A T E S

Niagara Falls is the largest waterfall in North America. It is made up of two waterfalls, the Horseshoe Falls and the American Falls.

Have you been to
Mount St. Helens?
It is in Washington.

★ **Mount
St. Helens**

UNITED STATES

Mount St. Helens is a volcano. It erupted in 1980 forming a crater on top.

Have you been to
Mammoth Cave?
It is in Kentucky.

UNITED STATES
Mammoth Cave ★

Mammoth Cave is a huge underground cave. There are stalactites and underground lakes in the cave.

Have you been to the **Everglades**?
It is in Florida.

UNITED STATES

Everglades

The **Everglades** is a huge marsh. It is known as a river of grass.

Have you been to these famous places?

14

★ Mount St. Helens

★ Yellowstone
National Park

★ Niagara Falls

★ Grand Canyon

★ Mammoth Cave

★ Everglades

Index